MATT TALBOT

HOPE FOR ADDICTS

MORGAN COSTELLOE

First published 1987 by
Veritas Publications
7/8 Lower Abbey Street
Dublin 1
Ireland
Email publications@veritas.ie
Website www.veritas.ie

This edition publication 2001

Reprinted 2005

ISBN 1 85390 548 8

Cover portrait by Sean O'Sullivan. Printed with the kind permission of the Capuchin Fathers, Dublin.

Designed by Colette Dower
Printed in the Republic of Ireland by Paceprint Ltd, Dublin

Veritas books are printed on paper made from wood pulp of managed forests. For every tree felled, at least one tree is planted, thereby renewing natural resources.

In 1884 a series of disturbing rumours circulated in O'Meara's public house on Dublin's North Strand. The first held that 'Barney' Talbot, a long-established member of the drinking fraternity, had given up the drink. The second suggested that his friends in O'Meara's, with whom he shared his good fortune in better times, had brought about that traumatic change. The previous Saturday 'Barney' and his brother stood outside the public house. Both were penniless but afflicted with an excruciating thirst and no one invited them in. One customer had it on good authority that 'Barney' was so hurt by his rejection that he had gone to a priest and taken the pledge for three months.

All shuddered at the suffering inflicted on a friend, who found difficulty in abstaining for three hours. But there was general agreement that he would be back. He was as much part of O'Meara's as the wooden counter that supported him late every evening. Yes, he would be back and his friends would make recompense for that unfortunate omission on the previous Saturday.

But Matt Talbot, known to his drinking friends as 'Barney', did not return to O'Meara's. At that time he was a chronic alcoholic. His life was totally unmanageable. He was part of the drug culture of his day and today he would probably be a junkie. After a horrendous struggle he overcame his addiction through the grace of God. He 'kicked the habit'. More than that, many recovered addicts throughout the world claim him as their model because his programme of recovery is as relevant today as it was a hundred years ago. They see Matt as a providential figure raised by God. His success gives hope to addicts.

Poor Start

Matt was born a disadvantaged child on 2 May 1856 to Charles Talbot and his wife, Elizabeth. The family lived at Aldborough Court, within fifty yards of Aldborough Barracks, the largest barrack of British troops in the country. Matt was the second of twelve children, but only nine survived infancy and childhood. This was not surprising as Thomas Willis reported in the *Dublin Journal of Medical Science* 1845 that half the babies born in Dublin died before they were two years old.

The great celebrations that took place in the barracks that month had nothing to do with the birth of the little boy around the corner. The Crimean War had ended and the soldiers were returning home. In the long term, this added to the problems of the North Strand where Matt grew up. Many of the dispossessed people of Europe attached themselves to the victorious army. They hoped to settle in London, but the city authorities moved them on, giving them free passage to Dublin. Here they settled close to the army barracks on the North Strand where their friends, the soldiers, would save them from starvation with the odd pig's cheek and loaf of bread. In time, the district became a 'red light' area, due mainly to their presence.

Matt, however, had other problems closer to home. His father Charlie had a good permanent job with the Port and Docks Board. He was also very fond of drink, with the result that the family was always poor and condemned to live in squalid slums. Unable to pay the rent, even as weekly tenants, the family kept moving from one tenement to another. While they remained in the Summerhill/North Strand area, it was a steady slide down the social ladder; even by tenement standards. They were caught in a vicious circle.

Alcohol was a temporary release from the appalling housing conditions but the more they drank the less money they had to improve themselves. The habit of heavy drinking passed from father to sons, and many years later, when most of the sons were working, the family were living at 5 Love Lane, Ballybough. The name of the district spoke for itself. Ballybough — in Irish, Baile na mBocht — meaning the 'town of the poor'. It was their worst slum dwelling.

Beggars and Paupers

Matt's Dublin of 1856 was an overcrowded city. Its population of a quarter of a million had been swollen by the famine refugees of the forties. These unfortunates had fled the countryside when the potato crop failed and sought work in vain in the cities. Many chose Dublin rather than New York, Boston or Liverpool. There were more than sixty thousand people in the Dublin hovels in laneways and side streets, so there was no room for the new arrivals.

The civic authorities adopted a radical solution. They built two work-houses, one on the northside where the Richmond Hospital stands today and one on the southside, on the present site of St James' Hospital. Each work-house accommodated four thousand paupers, men, women and children. They were given just enough food to save them from starvation. But there were still many beggars on the streets. A letter to the editor of the *Freeman's Journal* condemned the situation: the writer had walked across the city from Baggot

Street Bridge to Dorset Street, a distance of three miles, and was accosted by beggars eighty-seven times!

Slum Dwellings

The poor had to beg to survive. There were no social benefits like the dole, social assistance or sick benefit, which we take for granted. All the poor endured great hardship but those who were also old, or sick, faced destitution. To go to the workhouse was considered a disgrace, so the poor, in their charity, made space in their rooms for relatives and neighbours who had grown old and infirm.

Dr C. E. Orpen commented in the *Evening News* on 10 April 1832 that there were several hundred tenements in which eighty, ninety or a hundred people lived and some thousands accommodating forty or fifty. This meant that twelve and fourteen persons lived, ate and slept in the same room. The Talbots experienced this overcrowding as they moved from one tenement to another. These houses were mostly in a disgraceful condition.

This was highlighted by Mr Richard Martin, vice-chairman of the Artisans' Dwellings Company at the laying of the foundation stone of the new houses: 'At a recent Royal Sanitary Commission of Inquiry it was sworn in evidence, uncontradicted, and dwelt upon in the report, that one hundred thousand of the inhabitants of this city were living in abodes unfit for human habitation'. That statement was made in 1880, almost fifty years later, when there was a general improvement in the houses of the poor!

Health Hazards

There were many health hazards: badly constructed dwellings, poor ventilation, inadequate water supplies, narrow streets and the accumulation of filth around the houses. There were no lavatories, as we understand them, but each tenement was provided with a cess-pool in the back-yard where families emptied their slop buckets. As these often overflowed, health authorities later favoured an open sewer outside the tenements where water carried the waste to a central drain. Water was scarce also. Weekly tenants like the Talbots did not have running water in their house, but had to get it from a public tap. Even that was polluted. The canal company provided the city with water under contract in 1846. Thirteen years later it was discovered that this water was polluted.

The public health authorities were not unduly worried, as they considered that bad smell and not bad water was the real cause of fever (See S. E. Finer. *The Life and Times of Sir Edwin Chadwick,* p. 298). There were many bad smells. Those who drew drinking water form the river Poddle were in even greater danger. A reporter from the *Freeman's Journal,* accompanied by a doctor, gives us this startling account: 'In the neighbourhood of the Poddle is an open drain. It contains water which is little more than sewage, stagnant, sluggish, offensive in smell and appearance. A woman took a canful of water from this putrid stream, as we watched' (*Freeman's Journal,* 15 September 1871).

It was little wonder that Dublin experienced frequent serious epidemics of typhus, relapsing fever, typhoid, measles, scarletina, smallpox and, mainly because of the bad water, cholera as well. (Dr John Fleetwood, *History of Medicine in Ireland*).

Epidemics

A typhus epidemic lasted two years from 1817 to 1819 followed by serious cholera epidemics in 1831/32, 1849/49 and 1866. The first cholera attack devastated the city. At its height, 615 patients were admitted to the fever hospital in Grangegorman Lane in one day. It claimed 5,600 victims in one year, making the death rate five times worse than London, which had a similar epidemic in 1832.

While contagious diseases found most of their victims among the poor, they were no respecters of persons. Matt Talbot was baptised in the Pro-Cathedral on 5 May 1856 by Father James Mulligan, a young curate. The priest was dead within six weeks, having contracted a fever while ministering to sick parishioners.

There were many suggestions as to how the more affluent citizens should be protected against these recurring dangers. A radical proposal appeared in a 'Letter to the Editor' in the *Freeman's Journal* of 20 October 1826: 'I admit that, if you convert one quarter of the city into a great fever hospital and another into a poorhouse, you will meet the evil in the most effective way'.

Escape from Reality

But there could be no protection for those living in the slums. They were caught in the poverty trap. With little education and high unemployment, they had no hope of improving their social conditions. In the circumstances, alcoholic drink was the drug that gave them temporary release. It deadened their sense of privation and suffering and if one could afford sufficient quantities of it, it gave a sense of euphoria. The camaraderie of the public house compensated for the tension of the overcrowded tenements, and alcohol supplemented, to some degree, their diet of bread, buttermilk, fish and potatoes.

Mother Mary Aikenhead, the foundress of the Irish Sisters of Charity, observed this while visiting the poor in

Ringsend and Sandymount in 1833, the year after the great epidemic: 'The poor are inclined to indulge in spirituous liquor; they often resort to it in despair to drown the recollection of their sufferings. The small sum which will procure spirit is insufficient to provide a meal'.

To compound the situation further, workmen were paid their week's wages in pubs on Saturday mornings and were well advised to buy their foreman a drink if they wanted work on Monday. Jim Larkin, the famous labour leader, tackled this iniquitous practice many years later.

Social commentators of the last century concluded, almost unanimously, that poverty in Dublin was due to over-indulgence in drink. Very few drew the opposite conclusion: that over-indulgence in drink was due to poverty. This was much closer to the truth. One exception was Sir Charles Cameron, Dublin's Medical Officer of Health, who stated that in his opinion the poor drank heavily to escape from their condition and that the pub was the poor man's club.

Drinking Dublin

This need for drink generated business. There was a proliferation of pubs and shebeens throughout the city. In the early 1860s there were more than one thousand five hundred licensed premises in Dublin and just as many shebeens. Most grocery shops were licensed to sell drink for consumption, on condition that they provided a separate room off the premises for that purpose. The result was inevitable. Charlie Talbot, Matt's father, was not the only workman who drank heavily.

Modern scientific knowledge from the World Health Organisation informs us that one in every sixteen drinkers becomes an alcoholic, and there is no reason to believe that such was not the case in the last century. The drug culture of that day claimed its victims. There were more than sixteen thousand arrests for drunkenness in Dublin city in 1865. One third of them were women. Matters improved somewhat by the end of the century but by 1900, nine thousand persons were charged annually for drunkenness. The percentage of women was the same. Even today a man's status in a working-class area may be determined by his capacity 'to hold his drink' — the ability to drink a lot without showing signs of intoxication.

Some of the tradition is reflected in Dublin slang, where Eamonn Mac Thomais, an expert on the old city, tells us in his *Gur Cakes and Coal Blocks* that there are nineteen different expressions to describe a drunk person. They vary from the better known ones like 'stocious', 'plastered' and 'footless' to 'crooked' 'langers' and 'parlatic'.

THE 'MITCHER'

Matt Talbot grew up against that background of poverty and hopelessness. He went to school for the first time when he was eleven years old. It was long before the introduction of compulsory education and he really only enrolled in order to make his first Holy Communion and to receive the sacrament of Confirmation.

Education for the poor was generally considered to be an unnecessary luxury. It was no disgrace to be unable to read or write, since the tenement dwellers were condemned to life-long deprivation. Matt's older brother, John Joe, showed considerable academic promise and did well in later life. Matt hit the other extreme. To be fair, it was not all his fault. His father was still drinking heavily, so his mother went out to work as a charwoman to provide food for the family. Someone had to look after the babies while she was away and Matt accepted the responsibility willingly. He found himself caring for Robert (9), Mary (7), twin boys Edward and Charles who were five, Philip (3) who became the tough man of the family, Joseph (2) and Elizabeth, a baby a few months old.

But even when he was sent to school Matt did not always arrive. He played truant. After two troubled years Matt concluded his formal education. He could neither read nor write and his future in the over-loaded work market appeared bleak. The only impression he made on his teachers is recorded in the school roll-book of 1868. Beside his name in a column marked 'General Observations', Brother Ryan, his teacher, wrote: 'Mitcher'. No one could have guessed that this low-sized, illiterate thirteen-year old would become one of the most distinguished past pupils of O'Connell Schools.

The Black Stuff

Matt got a job as a messenger boy with the firm of E & J Burke Ltd, wine merchants. His wages were a pittance but they helped to ease the financial crisis at home. In retrospect, it is easy to see why this job was a disaster. Drinking was part of the sub-culture of the poor and there was 'the family failing' as seen in his father's heavy consumption.

E & J Burke's were more than just wine merchants. They bottled stout for the Guinness brewery and ale for Younger & Company of Edinburgh. Men sat all day tapping alcohol into bottles — boring, soul-destroying work, performed today by machines. We do not know if Matt was ever promoted to this position. His job was to deliver the finished product to public houses throughout the city. But there were always uncorked, half-empty bottles around.

They contained that curious, heavy, black liquid, which his father and other men enjoyed so much. Matt decided to take the first steps towards manhood. He started to drink.

CHANGE OF JOBS

It took Charlie two years to realise that he was not the only one in the family who was drinking. The unsteadiness he noticed in Matt was not, he convinced himself, due to his own inebriation. To his credit he took action to correct him: he gave Matt a beating and took him away from E & J Burke's to work beside himself at the bonded stores of Dublin's Custom House. He thought that he could keep a fatherly eye on him there, but events proved him wrong. Matt got a job as a messenger-boy, delivering bottles of whiskey to public houses, and proceeded to develop his taste for spirits.

Two years later he left that job to become a general labourer with Pemberton's, the building contractors. According to Mary, his sister, his father was pleased to see him leave. His constant drinking was disgracing Charlie. Together with his capacity to drink, Matt showed a tremendous capacity for work. He was small, tenacious and very strong and acquired the reputation of being a first-rate hodman. Unfortunately, the pattern of life that would plague him for the next twelve years was taking shape. He was progressively spending more money and time after hours in a local public house. 'Barney' Talbot was a regular patron of O'Meara's on the North Strand.

ADDICTION

His craving for alcohol gradually took over his life. He worked well when work was available but the purpose was to provide money for drink. At the end of the week he came home from O'Meara's with just a shilling to his mother. 'God forgive you, Matt,' she would say. 'Is that the way you treat your mother?' But days came when she did not get even that shilling. Matt left his entire wage in the public house and drew on it during the week. It did not always last that long, so he got drink on credit. This brought about the need for extra work to supplement his wages.

Matt was quite inventive. He walked to Baldoyle and Howth to mind horses while their owners drank in the local pubs and then returned to O'Meara's to spend his tips. That was a round trip of sixteen miles. He found extra jobs nearer home as well. Rosie Plunkett was the washerwoman in Aldborough Barracks nearby. She needed help to turn the mangle. Matt offered his service and got a pig's cheek for his trouble. That was sold to the highest bidder and he retired to enjoy the reward in O'Meara's. But sometimes he took more drastic measures. His sister, Susan, tells us that he sold his boots and shirt for drink.

The Fiddle

So far, Matt fed his addiction by keeping within the law, but that changed. He and his drinking friends began to steal a pig's cheek occasionally. The incident that caused him most distress, however, concerned a fiddle. One day a blind fiddler visited O'Meara's, played a few tunes for the patrons and had a few drinks from his takings. While he was drinking Matt and his brothers stole the poor man's fiddle. One of his drinking companions of those days, Pat Doyle, summed him up: 'He'd do anything for the drink'.

As a very old man, Pat met Mary Purcell while she researched her excellent biography, *Matt Talbot and his Times*. Matt's companions had many interests, like wrestling, playing cards, swimming, drink and girlfriends. Matt had only one: drink. For ten years his life was 'one long soak', to quote that biographer.

Today an alcoholic is a person whose life has become unmanageable on account of alcoholic drink. Had the term been in vogue in the 1880s, Matt Talbot would have qualified with flying colours!

Fateful Saturday

His drinking days came to a sudden end on a Saturday morning in 1884. Matt and his brother Phil, who was known for his fighting as well as his drinking, were unemployed. That did not deter them from going down to O'Meara's and waiting outside. It was an unwritten law among the drinking fraternity that a member with money to spare would help another who was down on his luck. Matt himself had done so. Undoubtedly, someone would come to his aid. But their friends passed them by and disappeared into the comfort of the pub. It was unbelievable, but true. The Talbot brothers might have been two lost animals for all they cared. Matt admitted later that he was cut to the heart.

After a while Phil walked away, but Matt retired to a nearby bridge and thought deeply about the rejection. He appeared to grasp suddenly and clearly the state of his life: a young man who had become a slave to drink, a person who had willingly endured great humiliation to satisfy his craving. The suddenness of his conversion has been compared with that of St Paul and St Augustine. The stubborn determination that characterised the rest of his life asserted itself: he would try to break the habit. He would take a pledge to abstain from alcohol for three months.

Had he foreseen the horrific consequences of this decision, as he fought the withdrawal symptoms over the next few months, he might have broken his resolution there and then and gone back to O'Meara's and begged his thoughtless friends for the price of a drink.

Fight-back

His mother could not believe it when Matt walked in. It was Saturday and he was sober. 'You're home early, Matt' she said, 'and you're sober!' After dinner he told her of his decision: 'I'm going to take the pledge, Ma!' But his mother was a realist. 'Go, in God's name', she advised him, 'but don't take it unless you are going to keep it'.

Matt went to Clonliffe College, the Dublin diocesan seminary, about a mile from his home. He asked to see a priest and went to Confession. He had been away from the sacrament for a number of years and while he never missed Sunday Mass — even though he regularly saw the priest and congregation through the haze of a hang-over — he had failed in other areas. It seems that his confessor gave him great encouragement. Matt took the pledge for three months. He left the College with a lighter step. The fight-back had begun.

Problems

Anyone who decides to overcome an addiction to alcohol faces certain immediate problems. First, he must avoid the temptation to drink. This meant that Matt Talbot could no longer visit O'Meara's, his haunt for twelve years. Phil, Joe and his other brothers went along, but he had to spend his evenings elsewhere. It meant also that he lost touch with his drinking companions, who remained convinced that 'Barney' would rejoin them some day.

Matt left O'Connell Schools an uneducated boy, but his response to his problems proved that, although he was still illiterate, he was an intelligent man. He went for a walk in the evenings away from the North Strand, heading westward towards the Phoenix Park. He got tired quickly so he rested in one of the churches on the way and said a few simple prayers for sobriety before making for home. Matt joined the Workingmen's Sodality in the local Jesuit church in Gardiner Street. This was a providential decision because the Sodality meetings not only filled in his evenings, but brought him in contact with its spiritual director, Father James Walshe SJ, an outstanding priest, who made a point of knowing personally every member of the Sodality. A kindly, understanding man, he became Matt's spiritual director, helping him to conquer his addiction, and fulfiling in many ways the role of a modern-day 'sponsor'.

Even before he met Father Walshe, Matt had decided that he needed spiritual help to keep his pledge for three months. He resolved to attend Mass and receive Holy Communion every morning at 5.00 a.m. before going to work. It was a revolutionary idea in 1884, when pious laymen went to Mass only on Sunday and received the Eucharist just twice a year. But Matt concluded that he needed all the help he could muster to overcome the pressure and temptation to return to the drink. How right he was!

Fearful Times

To see an addict in the throes of withdrawal is a frightening experience. The human body that is dependent on an addictive chemical substance can react violently when that substance is suddenly withdrawn. The common expression 'having the DTs' has been replaced in the popular vocabulary by the drug addict's 'cold turkey'. They both mean severe physical, emotional and psychological reactions — insomnia, shivering, shaking, nausea, hallucination, anxiety and depression.

Matt Talbot endured them all in the first weeks and months of his sobriety. He was virtually alone. No professional counselling was available. He depended on prayer and on Father Walshe's advice to remain sober. At times, close to despair, he remarked to his mother: 'I'll drink again when the three months are up'. At times he almost gave up. One evening, while out for his walk, he passed Bushe's public house at the corner of Gardiner Street and Dorset Street. Temptation struck. He walked up and down a few times feeling the money in his pocket. Then he went in to break his pledge. The public house was packed and the barman ignored the stranger while he served his regular customers. The snub was too much for Matt. He pulled himself together, left the bar and spent the rest of the evening in Gardiner Street church nearby, praying for the strength to remain sober.

As a result of that experience, he made a resolution that he kept for the rest of his life. He never carried money on his person. His reasoning was very simple: no money, no drink.

Waste of Time?

Another incident of note took place on a Sunday morning in the Jesuit church, Gardiner Street. He attended the 6.30 a.m. Mass and was struck by a violent sense of hopelessness as he approached the altar rails to receive Holy Communion. He felt certain that he would drink again and that all his prayers and good intentions were hypocrisy and waste of time. He left the church. Matt spent most of that morning going from church to church seeking consolation. Eventually he returned to Gardiner Street church and received the Eucharist at a later Mass.

The memory of such experiences remained with him all his life. As an old man, he told his sister: 'Susan, never be too hard on a man who can't give up drink. It's as hard to give up drink as it is to raise the dead to life'. But he did give up the drink. Thanks to the grace of God, his own stubborn tenacity and a strict programme of rehabilitation, he remained sober until his death forty-one years later.

After the initial period he renewed his pledge for another three months, then for a year, and finally took it for life. When a Jesuit priest, Father John Cullen, who was attached to Gardiner Street church, founded the Pioneer Total Abstinence Association in 1890, Matt became one of its first members.

Alcoholics Anonymous

Matt Talbot's recovery might have been just one man's victory over overwhelming odds until the foundation of Alcoholics Anonymous (AA) in the United States in 1935. It gave it a new significance. AA is a non-sectarian fellowship of men and women who share their experience, strength and hope with each other that they may solve their common problem and help others to recover from alcoholism. The only requirement for membership is a desire to stop drinking. Its description of an alcoholic is 'a person whose drinking causes a continuing and progressive problem in any of the following areas of his, or her, life: physical or mental health, marriage, relationships with others, finances or job'. You do not have to be on 'skid row' to qualify.

As AA sees it, alcoholism is an illness. The alcoholic cannot control his drinking because he is ill in his body and in his mind. In other words, his chemical dependency on the drug, ethyl alcohol, is a three-fold illness: physical, psychological and spiritual. It develops almost unnoticed over a number of years in the individual. It can be prevented, but its progress cannot be arrested until the alcoholic recognises his, or her, illness. AA went on to produce a self-help recovery programme — its famous 'Twelve Steps'. No other programme can claim such a success rate from addiction.

The idea of conversion is central to this programme. As the alcoholic is powerless to help himself, he must turn to a power higher than himself for strength and hand his life over to the care of God, as he understands him. This is another expression of the age-old Christian ideal of conversion, 'metanoia' — turning away from self-worship and turning back to God. Several years later when the 'Twelve Steps' programme was well established, some members of AA in the United States made an historic discovery: a recovering alcoholic, named Matt Talbot, had stumbled upon their programme fifty years previously. He had practised almost all the 'Twelve Steps' and his conversion was so complete that he was a candidate for canonisation by the Catholic Church.

The Twelve Steps

The following is the 'Twelve Steps' programme of Alcoholics Anonymous:

1. *We admit we are powerless over alcohol — that our lives have become unmanageable.*
2. *Come to believe that a Power greater than ourselves could restore us to sanity.*

3. *Make a decision to turn our will and lives over to the care of God as we understand him.*
4. *Make a searching and fearless moral inventory of ourselves.*
5. *Admit to God, to ourselves and to another human being the exact nature of our wrongs.*
6. *Be entirely ready to have God remove all these defects of character.*
7. *Humbly ask him to remove our shortcomings.*
8. *Make a list of all persons we have harmed and become willing to make amends to them all.*
9. *Make direct amends to such people, wherever possible, except where to do so would injure them or others.*
10. *Continue to take personal inventory and, when we are wrong, promptly admit it.*
11. *Seek through prayer and meditation to improve our conscious contact with God, as we understand him, praying only for knowledge of his will for us and the power to carry it out.*
12. *Having had a spiritual awakening as a result of these steps, we try to carry this message to alcoholics and practise principles in all our affairs.*

The fourth, fifth and eleventh steps emphasise, in particular, the need for spiritual rehabilitation.

First Step

'We admit we are powerless over alcohol – that our lives have become unmanageable.'

His powerlessness over alcohol hit Matt hard on the day he took the pledge. There was no denying his insatiable thirst. Many diverse images from the past proved that: a blind man's fiddle, horses outside a pub, shirts and vests emerging from a mangle, pigs' cheeks dripping brine, a pawn shop, a shilling for his mother. He had to have money to feed his addiction. The grace of God tore away his mask of self-deception. He was no longer in charge of his own life. Drink was his master. He was its slave. He would break the shackles. He would show his so-called friends in O'Meara's that he did not need their money. But he had to prove himself to himself first.

Second Step
'Come to believe that a Power greater than ourselves could restore us to sanity.'

Matt had no difficulty in identifying his 'Higher Power'. He had become careless about his reception of Holy Communion and the Sacrament of reconciliation, but otherwise he was a practising Catholic. He never missed Sunday Mass, no matter what his condition might be from the night before. He always said a 'Hail Mary' — the prayer to the Mother of God — before he flopped into bed.

He had heard hundreds of sermons over the years and the repetition of many scriptural texts convinced him that the God he believed in from childhood would help him now. How often had he heard the words of Jesus quoted in the long half-hour sermons of those days? 'Come to me, all who labour and and heavy laden and I will give you rest for your souls' (Mk 11:29), 'I had said this to you, that in me you may have peace', 'In the world you have tribulation; be of good cheer, I have overcome the world' (Jn 16:33). Then there was the much-quoted assurance, which God gave St Paul: 'My grace is sufficient for you, for my power is made perfect in weakness' (2 Cor 12:9).

When Matt was drunk he lost his reason, but he never lost his faith. He did not desert God in his addiction and God did not desert him in his crisis. The Holy Spirit was prompting him. Matt found his 'Higher Power' quickly. Within a few hours of his conversion, he was on his way to Clonliffe College.

Third Step

'Make a decision to turn our will and lives over to the care of God as we understand him.'

A good Confession means turning away from sin and turning one's will back to God. From the moment Matt Talbot went to Confession that Saturday he stood unflinchingly by that decision. He had a fierce struggle ahead but God would see him through. He turned to daily mass and reception of the Eucharist. He would survive from one encounter with Christ to another — an early form of 'one day at a time'. He dropped into a church in the evening to renew his strength by prayer and thank the Lord for another day without a drink. These were the early days of his conversion. Later he expanded his spiritual programme to imitate the rule of the early Irish monks.

Fourth Step

'Make a searching and fearless moral inventory of ourselves.'

Many recovering alcoholics find this and the Fifth Step very difficult. It was part of Matt's preparation for that Confession in Clonliffe College and for subsequent ones, as it was impossible to complete the inventory at short notice. It appears that Matt met a kind and understanding confessor in Clonliffe College that Saturday afternoon and he surely helped him in his preparation.

A penitent is required to confess all his serious sins number and kind — in so far as he can remember — in order to receive absolution. If he cannot recall them all, as happened in Matt's case, he is expected to do his best and mention any other serious offences which he might remember later, in subsequent confessions. Father James Walshe, whom Matt chose as his spiritual director, would help with these. But certain failings in justice would stand out in his mind that Saturday — unpaid debts and sins against justice, against his mother and the blind fiddle player. His confessor would have reminded him that these required restitution whenever Matt was in a position to make it.

Fifth Step
'Admit to God, to ourselves and to another human being the exact nature of our wrongs.'

As we have seen, all this is included in 'going to Confession', or receiving the Sacrament of Reconciliation as it is usually described today. It takes humility and courage to see ourselves as we really are and to admit it to God and to ourselves. Matt took that step. The 'other human being' in this case was a Catholic priest. To outsiders he is an ordained professional advisor, but to Catholics, like Matt, he is more. He is a servant of God with the authority to forgive sins, to bring pardon and peace to anyone who is sincerely repentant and intends to reform. His task is to understand, to make allowance and to show God's love, compassion and mercy to the person who kneels before him.

Sixth Step
'Be entirely ready to have God remove all these defects of character.'

Receiving that sacrament was not just a forgiveness or a cleansing for Matt. There was that aspect to it: 'Though your sins are like scarlet they shall be as white as snow' (Is 1:18). But the Sacrament of Reconciliation was also the source of divine power that enabled him to reform his life. It spelt out that, with God's help, it was possible to rebuild his life, to start again, to face the future with hope. There would be no instant solution. A long struggle lay ahead, but taking one day at a time, all things are possible with God. Matt began the practice of attending daily Mass that weekend. It lasted for more than forty years.

Seventh Step

'Humbly ask him to remove our shortcomings.'

Pat Doyle was asked for his abiding memory of his former drinking companion, Matt Talbot. 'He couldn't go easy at anything', he replied. It was a very good description. Matt's insatiable thirst for drink was now converted into an all-absorbing drive for closer union with God. Once his initial struggle for sobriety was over he pursued this quest relentlessly for the rest of his life. Asking God to remove his failings was only the first step on the way. He chose the rule of the early Irish monks. It was summarised by St Columbanus: 'Pray daily, fast daily, work daily, study daily'.

It was a well-tested way to God that produced many saintly men and women, but its emphasis on penance would scare many modern Christians. Not so Matt Talbot. In stature and approach he resembled the monks of the sixth century. He left home, found a tenement flat where he could live a solitary life, taught himself to read and write and chose a spiritual director who guided him in his quest.

Eighth and Ninth Steps

'Make a list of all persons we have harmed and become willing to make amends to them all.'

'Make direct amends to such people, wherever possible, except where to do so would injure them or others.'

During his drinking days Matt borrowed and scrounged money. After his conversion he spent a long time repaying his debts. The fiddle, which he stole from the blind man, was another matter. Matt never saw him again. He made enquiries and called to the city poorhouses, but to no avail. Finally, Matt concluded that he was unlikely ever to find him. He was probably dead, so Matt gave a priest the price of the fiddle to have Masses celebrated for the blind man.

Matt often left his mother short of money when he was drinking. He compensated her in a different way. When his father, Charlie, died, he brought her to live with him in his tenement flat and looked after her until she died thirteen years later. She alone saw him praying into the early hours of the morning. One of his sorrows was that neither he, nor the family, could afford to buy a grave when she died and she was buried in the Paupers' Plot in Glasnevin cemetery.

But if Matt offended against justice in early life, he made amends later. He gave away phenomenal amounts of money in almsgiving as part of his spiritual programme. From a wage packet of £3.50, he would give away £3 and keep the rest for food, heating and rent. He helped destitute neighbours, fellow workers, charitable institutions and a missionary society. His contributions went to the Poor Clares in Keady, County Armagh, and Father Drumgoole's orphanages in New York. On one occasion he embarrassed a priest who called into T & C Martin's collecting for a new church in County Monaghan. Matt gave him his wage packet unopened. Susan, his sister, commented: 'He had no time for money'.

Tenth Step
'Continue to take personal inventory and when we are wrong, promptly admit it'.

Many Catholics conduct an examination of conscience before retiring at night and then recite a prayer of sorrow to God for their offences during the day. Matt, as a member of the Third Order of St Francis, which he joined in 1890, was well aware of this simple spiritual exercise and almost certainly practised it every day. It was also a preliminary to his weekly confession. His niece, Annie Johnson, tells us that 'Matt would tell you straight out what he thought of you, but he would try not to hurt your feelings'. She goes on; 'If ever he had hot words with men at work he would go afterwards and apologise to them'.

Eleventh Step
'Seek through prayer and meditation to improve our conscious contact with God, as we understand him, praying only for knowledge of his will for us and the power to carry it out'.

Matt's return to prayer after many years promised little — a plea from the heart for the strength to abstain from drink. But it gathered momentum. Eventually the companionship of his friends in O'Meara's was replaced by the companionship of Christ in the Blessed Eucharist. He spent hours in a church on Sunday, kneeling upright in an obscure corner without support, oblivious of activity around him.

On a weekday he went to mass and Communion early, called into a church for a moment on his way to work and again on the way home. After his evening meal he attended a Sodality meeting and retired to his flat to pray before going to bed. He visited his spiritual director once a week and, thanks to him, Matt became a master of prayer who understood that the secret of true holiness was the acceptance of God's Will in his life. He died in 1925 on his way to Mass in the forty-first year of his sobriety.

It is interesting that during those years he managed to conceal his ascetical life from his fellow workers in T & C Martin's. He was popular and avoided ostentation. Daniel Manning, who knew him well, said that he was 'always mild and agreeable and gentle, good-humoured and easy to get on with'. His inner peace appealed to Paddy Laird, a friend of his, who said, 'Matt smiled at everything except a dirty joke'.

Twelfth Step

'Having had a spiritual awakening as a result of these steps, we try to carry this message to alcoholics and practise principles in all our affairs'.

There is no evidence that Matt set out to carry his message of total abstinence to alcoholics. He was an 'easy touch' for money. Many a worker in T & C Martin's got a loan of money from him and if Matt thought that their financial difficulty was due to over-indulgence in drink, he would advise them kindly to take a pledge. He would add that he had been 'an awful man for drink' and only found peace of mind when he gave it up.

There was one humourous exception to his general policy. Soon after taking the pledge he invited Pat Doyle, his former drinking companion, for a walk. Without realising where they were going, Pat suddenly found himself in the grounds of Clonliffe College. Matt approached a priest who was walking in the grounds and said: 'Here he is for you now Father, I've brought him to take the pledge'. When Pat realised the danger he fled through the gate! Such imprudent zeal did not manifest itself again.

Why Drugs?

The 'Twelve Steps' programme has been highly successful throughout the world. The recognition of a spiritual dimension makes sense, for it has been said that when a person turns to drugs, or to excessive drinking, he is seeking happiness, and in that sense he is really seeking God. Only faith in Him can fully satisfy that desire. In fact the problem is a modern expression of St Augustine's remark: 'You made us for yourself O Lord and our hearts are restless until they rest in you' — and he spoke from considerable personal experience!

Many addicts have a low self-image. Sadly, they do not realise that every person is precious to God and has been redeemed by the blood of Christ. Pain, loss, or rejection is often behind an addiction and this brings us to the mystery of suffering. Acceptance can come by realising that all suffering acquires value when united with Christ's Passion. The Paschal Mystery — the suffering, death and resurrection of Jesus — tells us that pain, loss and rejection can bring us closer to God.

The lives of outstanding recovered alcoholics and drug addicts are proof that many of the psychological factors that affect alcoholics could benefit from a 'faith' prescription also. American authorities on alcoholism hold that the following psychological traits are commonly found in alcoholics:

1. A high level of anxiety in interpersonal relations
2. Emotional immaturity
3. Ambivalence towards authority
4. Low frustration tolerance
5. Low self-esteem
6. Perfectionism
7. Guilt
8. Feelings of isolation

Matt Talbot Retreat Movement

The credit for discovering that Matt Talbot practised almost all the 'Twelve Steps' within his recovery programme goes to the Matt Talbot Retreat Movement of the United States. It was founded in May 1942 as a non-profit corporation by a small number of recovering alcoholics. They were all members of Alcoholics Anonymous and were making a retreat at a Jesuit Retreat House in New Jersey. They had retired for a few days to work on the spiritual steps of their programme.

The aim of the Movement is to assist alcoholics in their spiritual rehabilitation with special reference to the Fourth, Fifth and Eleventh Steps. It is confined at present to men and women who are members of the Fellowship of AA. It is not, and cannot be, affiliated to AA, however, and remains a back-up service to its members, regardless of sex, nationality or creed. The secondary aim of the Movement is to promote the cause of its patron, Matt Talbot. At the time of writing, the Movement has twenty-five thousand members in one hundred groups in the United States and Canada. A branch of the Retreat Movement, the first in Europe, was established in Ireland in 1998.

Remembering Old Friends

The story of Matt Talbot has been an inspiration to its members for almost fifty years. They can identify with him easily. He understands their problems. For he was not just an alcoholic whose illness brought suffering to himself and his family, but he later saw one of his brothers die from the effects of excessive drinking. Matt's recovery shows that the conversion demanded by the 'Twelve Steps' programme is possible, even to the stage where the recovered addict becomes a candidate for canonisation.

Similar programmes are now used for the rehabilitation of men and women addicted to other drugs such as heroin, LSD and 'crack'. The Catholic Church has no patron saint for addicts at present and members of the Retreat Movement hope that Matt Talbot will fill that vacancy some day. Their claims that they have received many graces through his intercession are borne out by favours reported from many countries. The vast majority of them concern the grace of conversion of alcoholics and the comfort of their families in countries as far apart as Ireland and India, the United States and Australia, Great Britain and Guatemala.

It appears that 'Barney' Talbot, a former patron of O'Meara's pub, has not forgotten the drinking fraternity in death.

Begin Again!

This booklet is not intended to be a biography of Matt Talbot. It sets out to show that he was born into a sub-culture where drinking alcohol was almost inevitable. But, having become an addict, he fought his addiction primarily with a spiritual programme and recovered.

Two full-length biographies: *Matt Talbot and his Times* by Mary Purcell (Franciscan Herald Press) and *Matt Talbot* by Joseph Glynn (Veritas) give a comprehensive account of his life. A booklet, *The Mystery of Matt Talbot* by Fr Morgan Costelloe (Messenger Publications), explains the ascetical programme he adopted, based on the Rule of the Irish monks.

The fact that he practised almost all of the 'Twelve Steps' of the Alcoholics Anonymous programme fifty years before they were conceived makes Matt Talbot a prophetic figure. His successful recovery gives hope to addicts while highlighting the need for a spiritual dimension in their rehabilitation.

Addiction to drugs — from alcohol to heroin — is unfortunately worldwide, but the story of Matt Talbot spells out that, with the grace of God, it is possible to realise the advice of the late Cardinal O'Connell of Boston:

'Tire not of new beginnings...
Build thy life — never upon regret
Always upon resolve!
Shed no tears on the blotted page of the past
But turn the leaf and smile...
To see the clean white virgin page
Before thee... **BEGIN AGAIN!**

Prayer for the Canonisation of Matt Talbot

Lord, in your servant Matt Talbot you have given us a wonderful example of triumph over addiction, of devotion to duty, and of lifelong reverence for the Most Holy Sacrament. May his life of prayer and penance give us courage to take up our crosses and follow in the footsteps of Our Lord and Saviour, Jesus Christ.

Father, if it be your will that your beloved servant should be glorified by your Church, make known by your heavenly favours the power he enjoys in your sight. We ask this through the same Jesus Christ Our Lord. Amen.

Matt Talbot's tomb is in Our Lady of Lourdes Church, Sean McDermott Street, Dublin 1. Anyone who receives a favour through his intercession is requested to write to Fr Morgan Costelloe, Vice-Postulator of the Cause, c/o the above named church.